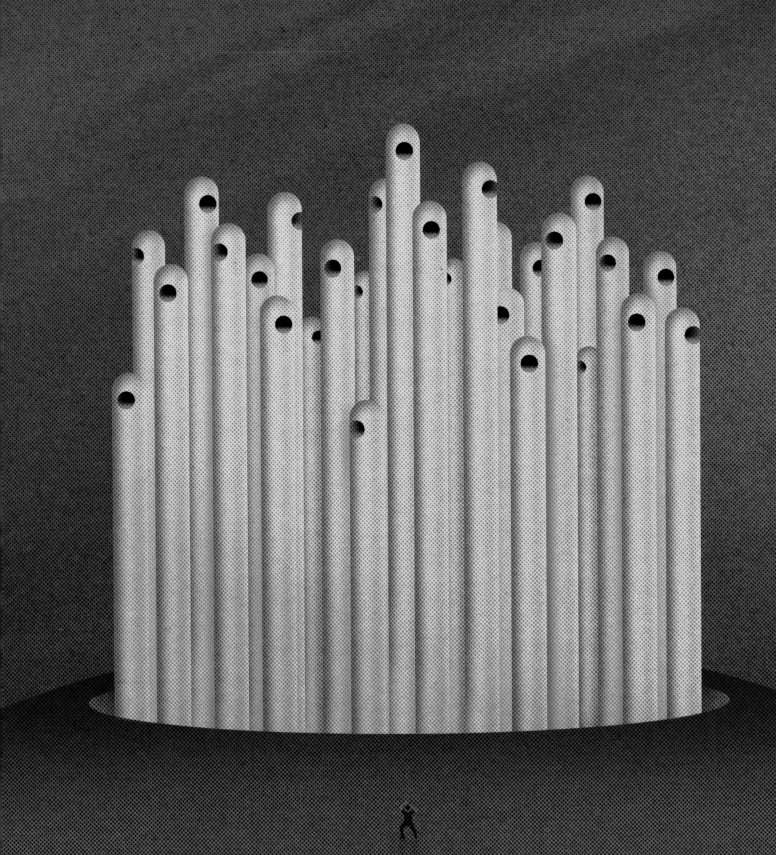

Produced by
Alfred Music Publishing Co., Inc.
P.O. Box 10003
Van Nuys, CA 91410-0003
alfred.com

Printed in USA

ISBN-10: 0-7390-6849-0
ISBN-13: 978-0-7390-6849-6

Arranged by Olly Weeks
Edited by Lucy Holliday

Artwork by www.laboca.co.uk
Photography by Danny Clinch

musemanagement.co.uk
muse.mu

UPRISING

Words and Music by Matthew Bellamy

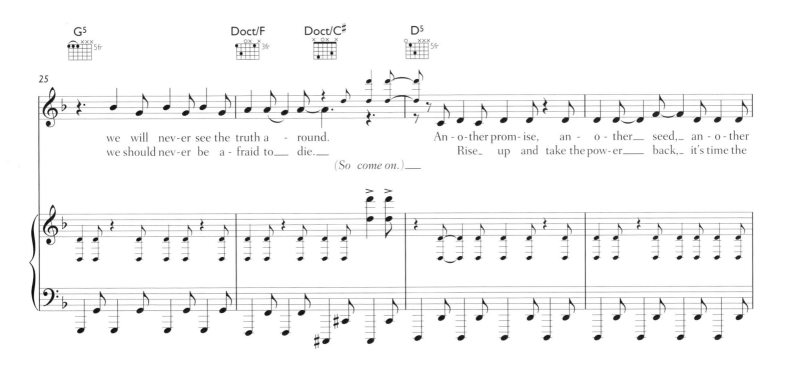

pack -aged lie to keep us trapped in____ greed, and all the
fat cats had a heart at - tack,__ they know that

green__ belts wrapped a -
their__ time's com - ing

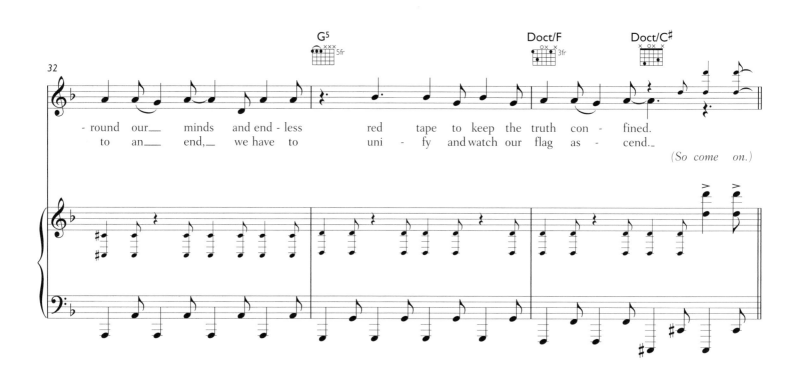

- round our__ minds and end - less red tape to keep the truth con - fined.
to an__ end,__ we have to uni - fy and watch our flag as - cend..

(So come on.)

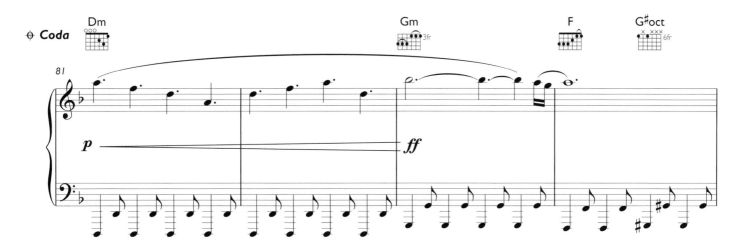

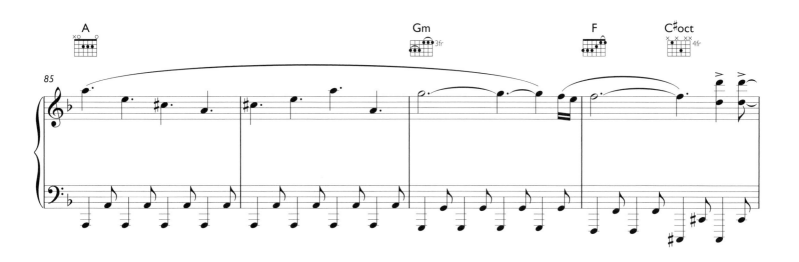

RESISTANCE

Words and Music by Matthew Bellamy

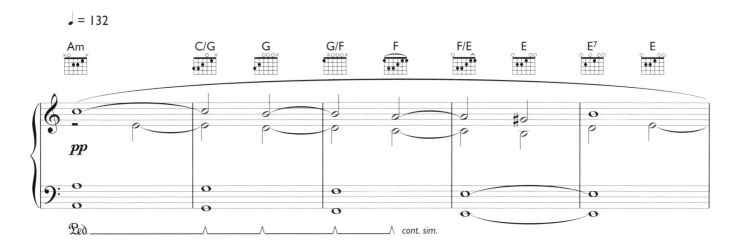

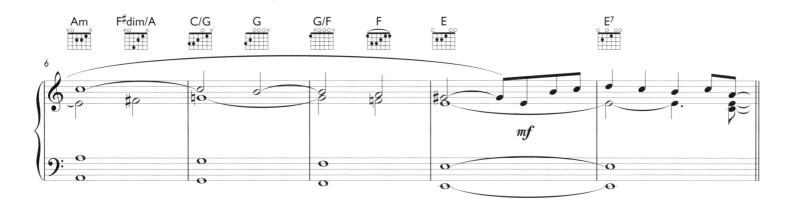

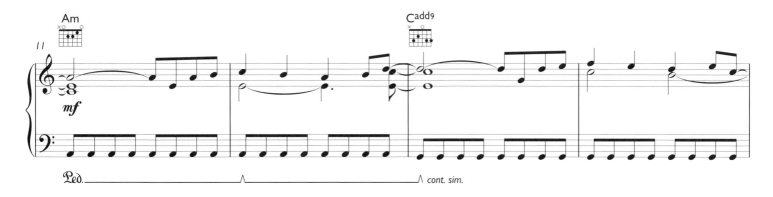

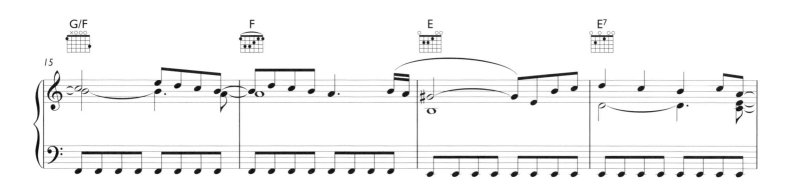

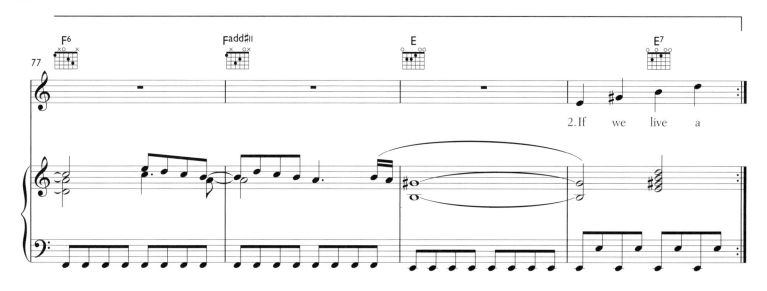

2.If we live a

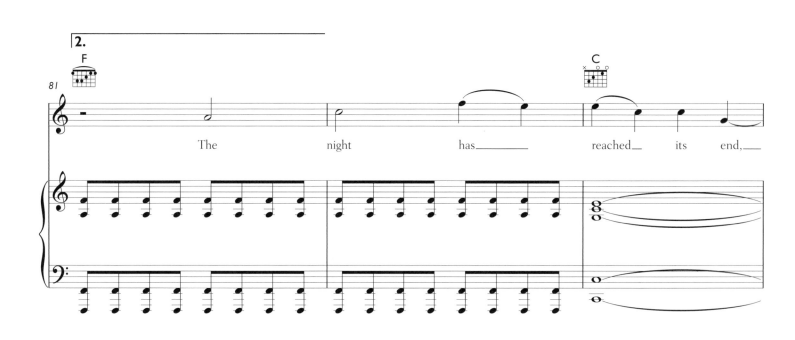

The   night   has   reached   its   end,

_____ we   can't   pre - tend,   we must

UNDISCLOSED DESIRES

Words and Music by Matthew Bellamy

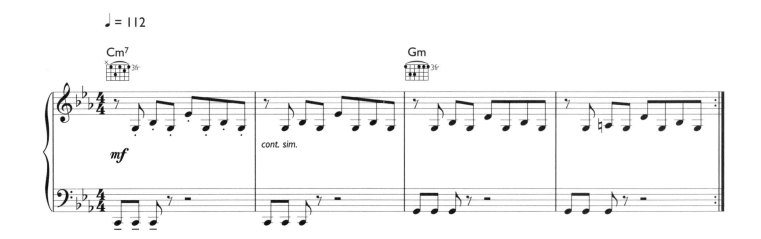

1. I know you've suf-fered but I don't want you to hide,
2. You trick your lov-ers that you're wick-ed and di-vine,

it's cold and love-less, I won't let you be de-nied.
you may be a sin-ner but your in-no-cence is mine.

(1.) Sooth - ing, _____ I'll make _____ you feel pure, _____
(2, %) Please _____ me, _____ show _____ me how it's done, _____

trust _____ me, _____ you _____ can _____ be sure. _____
tease _____ me, _____ you _____ are _____ the one. _____

I want to re-con-cile _____ the vio-lence in your heart, _____

D.% al Coda

ooh.

Coda

vocals 2° only

Mmm,

(Play small notes 2°)

mf

mmm.

N.C.

UNITED STATES OF EURASIA (+ COLLATERAL DAMAGE)

Words and Music by Matthew Bellamy

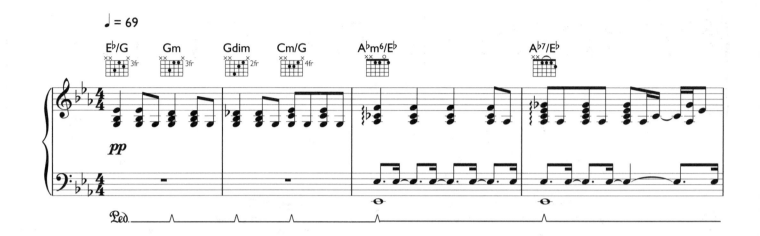

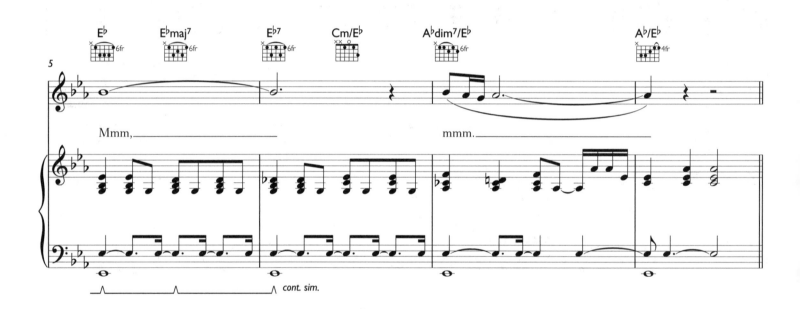

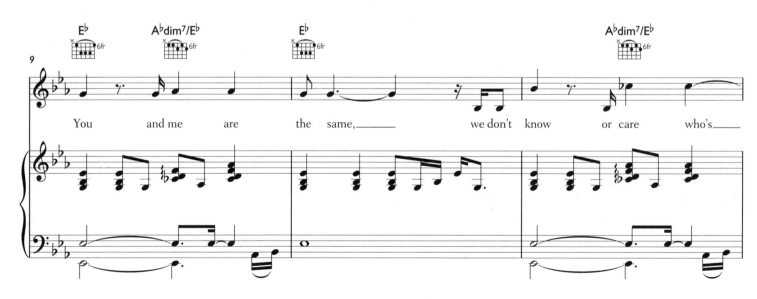

Mmm,_____ mmm._____

You and me are the same,_____ we don't know or care who's_____

GUIDING LIGHT

Words and Music by Matthew Bellamy

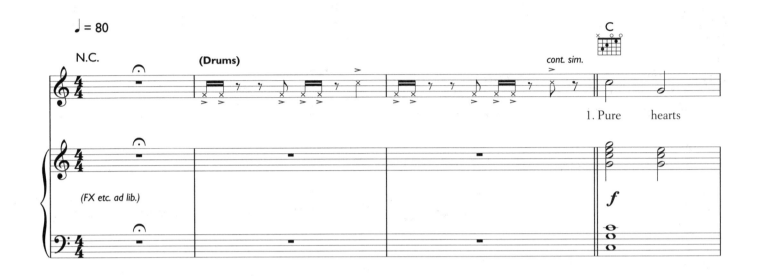

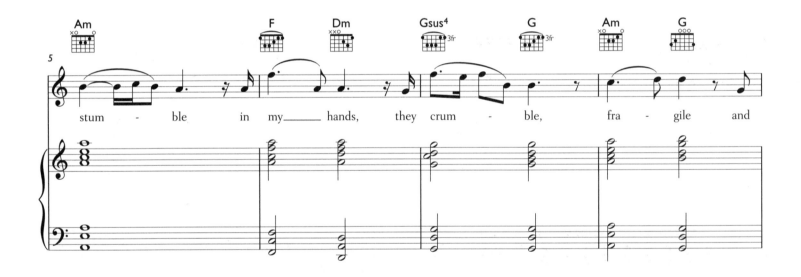

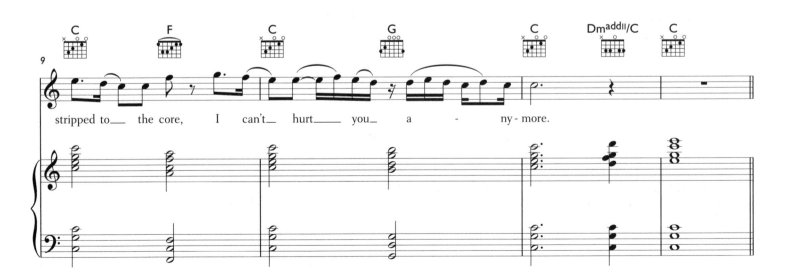

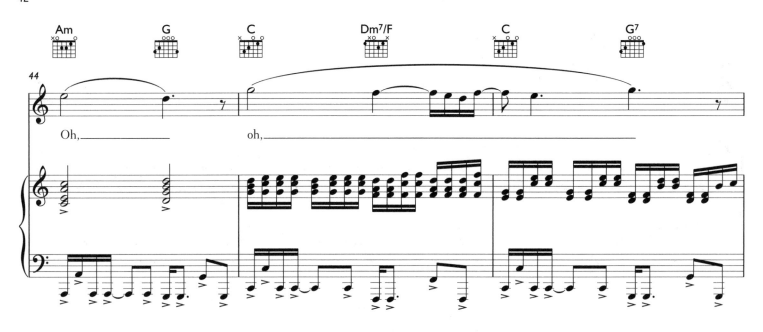

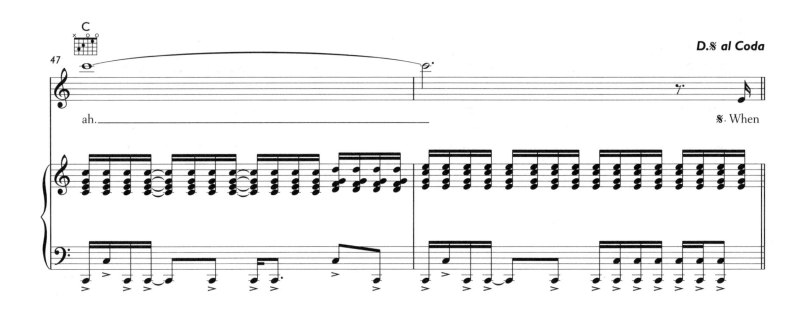

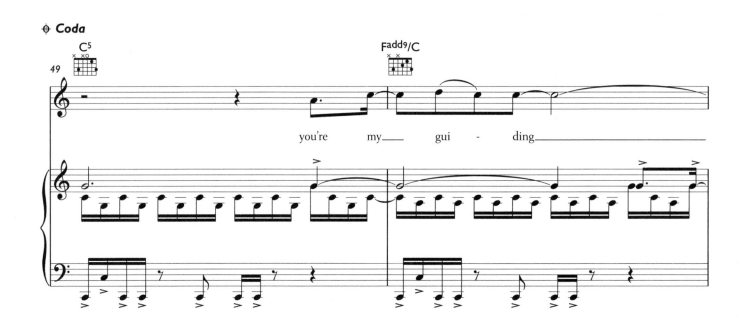

UNNATURAL SELECTION

Words and Music by Matthew Bellamy

1. I am hun - gry_____ for some un - rest,_____ I want to push this be - yond__ a peace - ful pro - test.
2. No re - li - gion or mind_ vi - rus,_____ is there a hope that the facts__ will ev - er find us?

No hope for fate, it's un-na-tu-ral se-lec-tion
No hope for fate, it's a ran-dom chance se-lec-tion

(Ah.)
(Hey! Hey! Hey!)

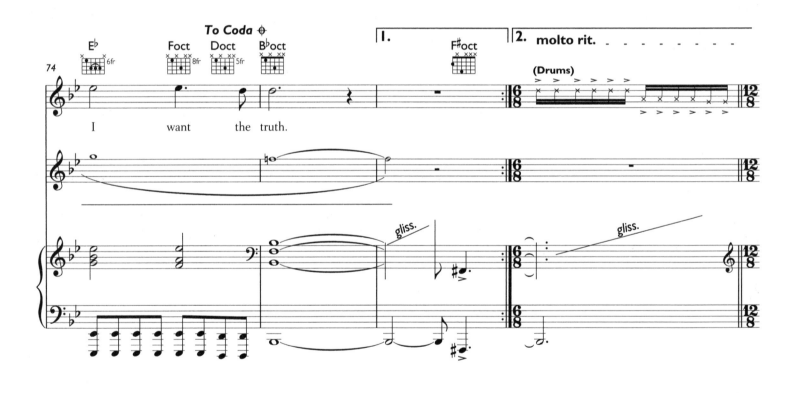

I want the truth.

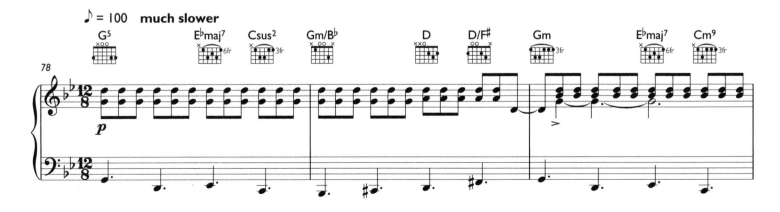

MK ULTRA

Words and Music by Matthew Bellamy

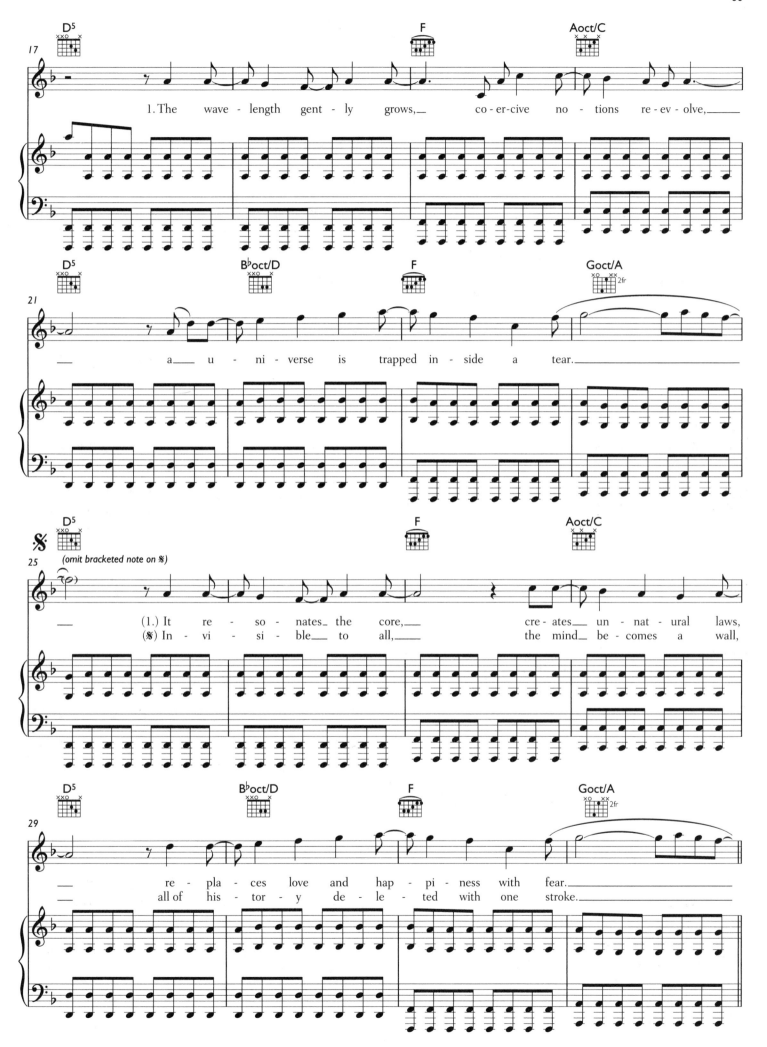

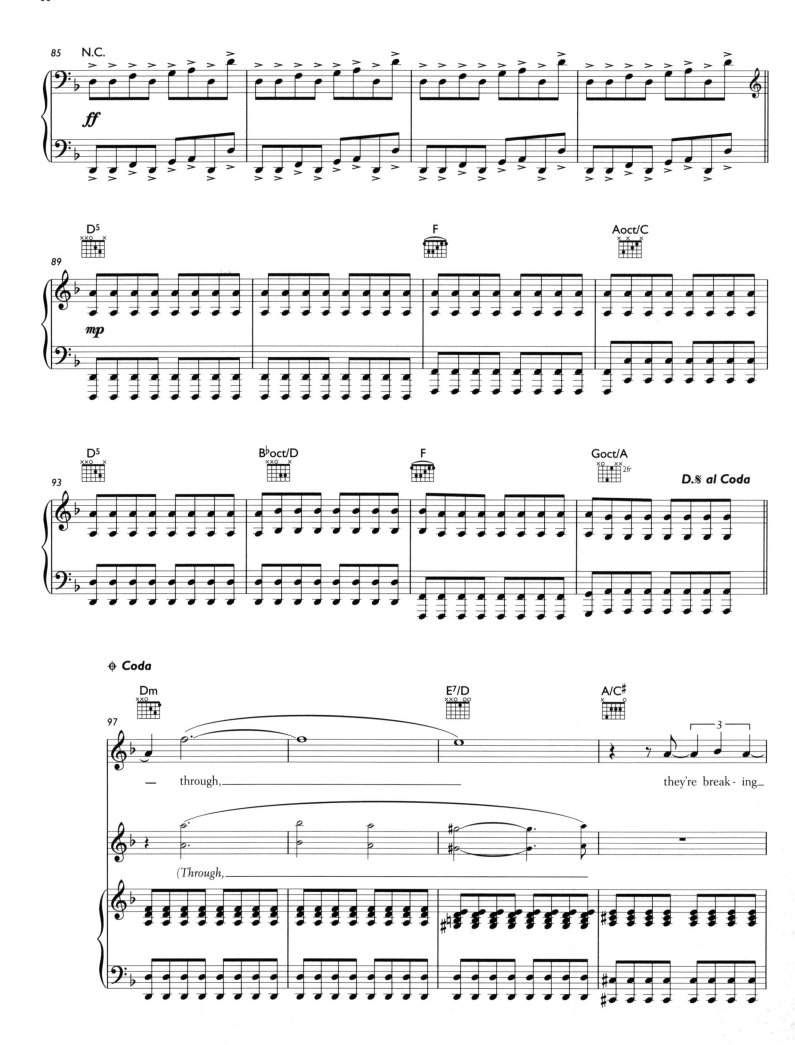

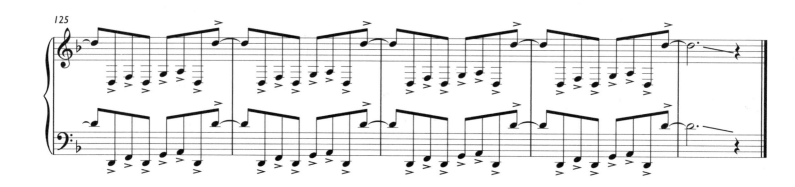

I BELONG TO YOU (+ MON CŒUR S'OUVRE À TA VOIX)

Words and Music by Matthew Bellamy

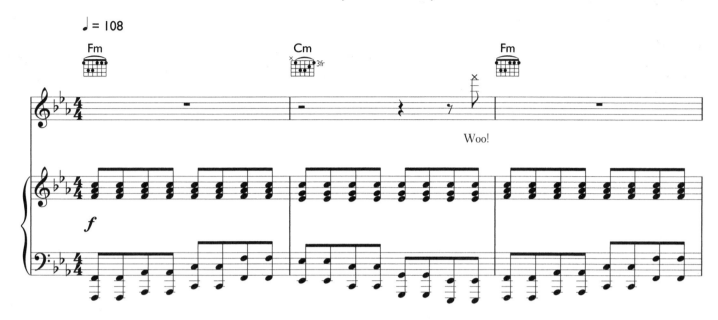

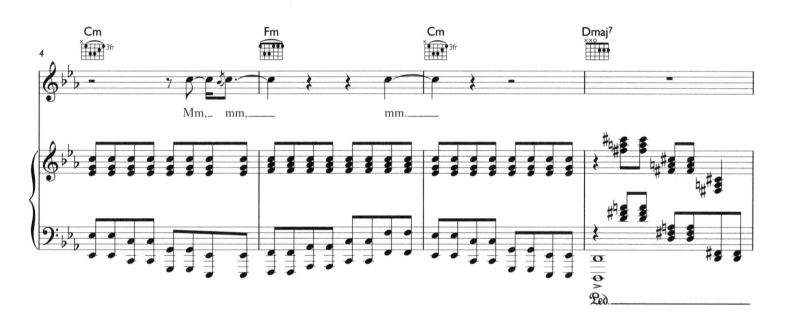

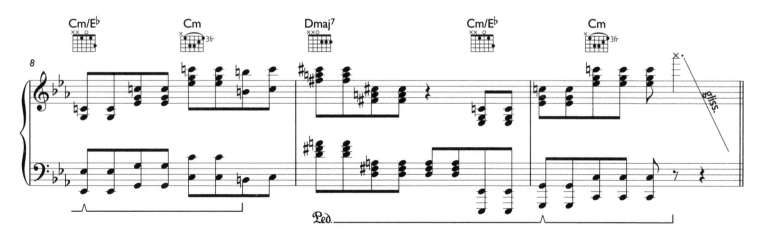

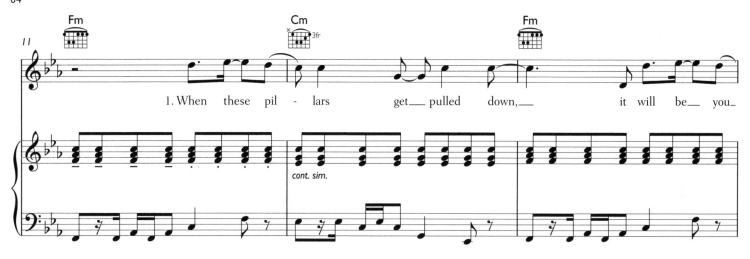

1. When these pil - lars get pulled down, it will be you

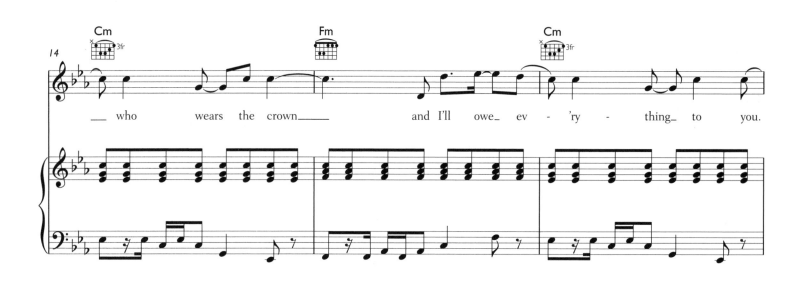

who wears the crown and I'll owe ev - 'ry - thing to you.

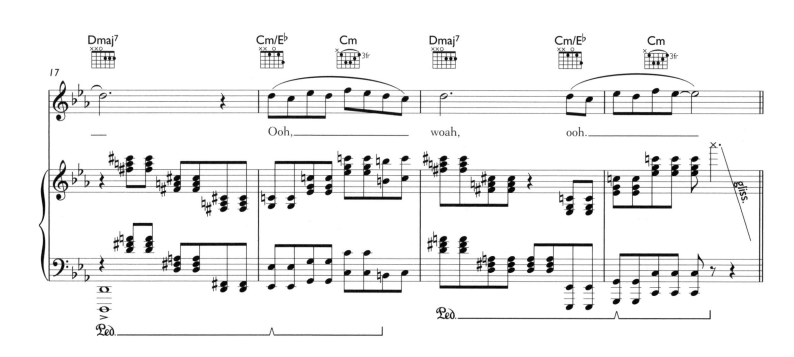

Ooh, woah, ooh.

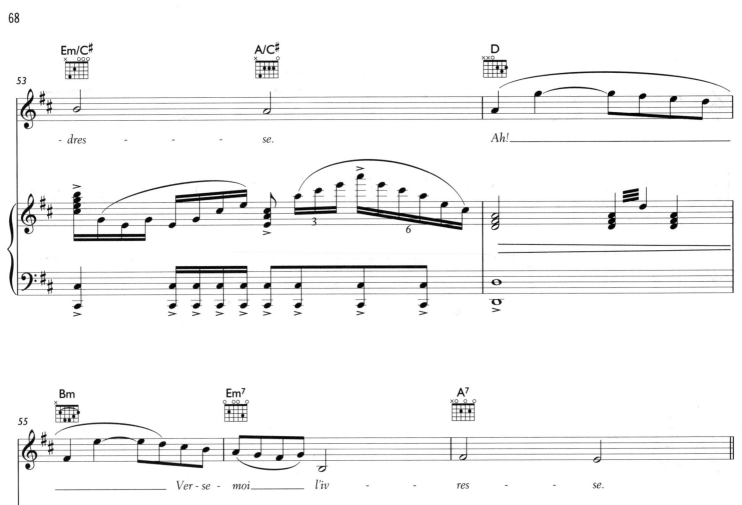

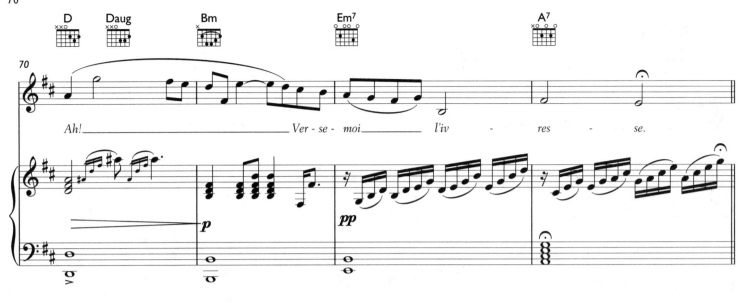

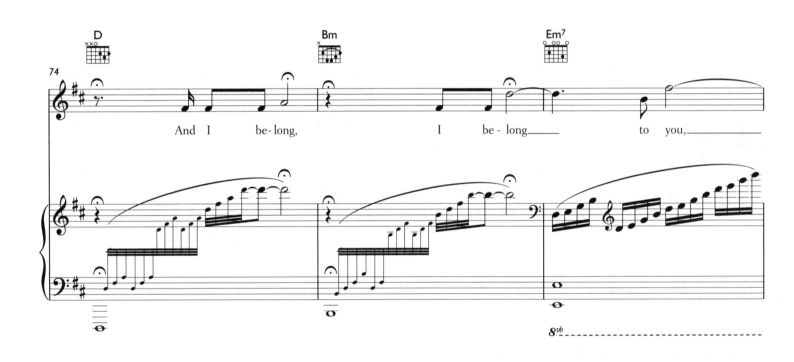

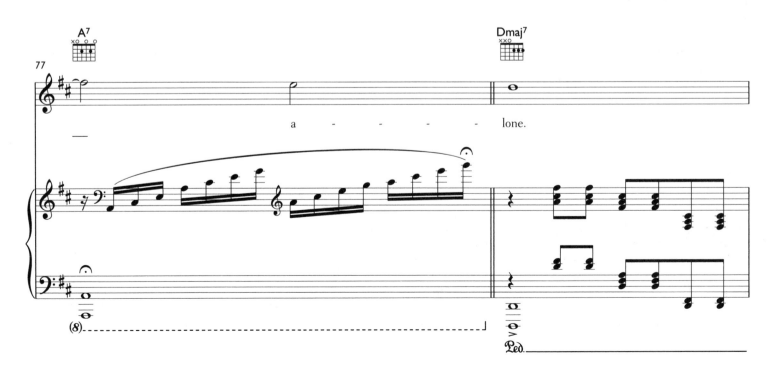

EXOGENESIS: SYMPHONY PART I (OVERTURE)

Words and Music by Matthew Bellamy

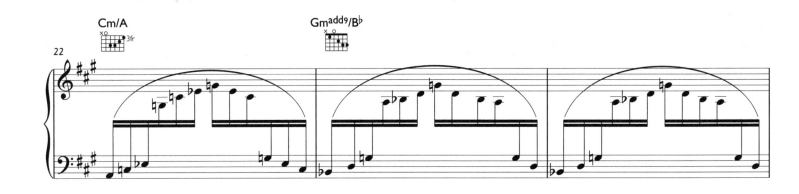

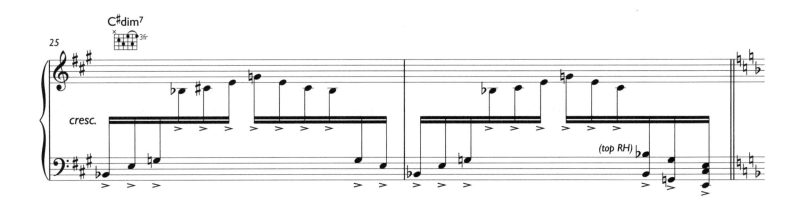

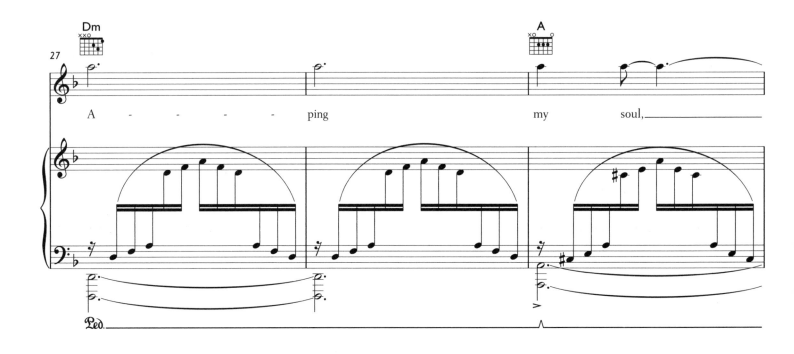

A - - - - ping   my   soul,_____

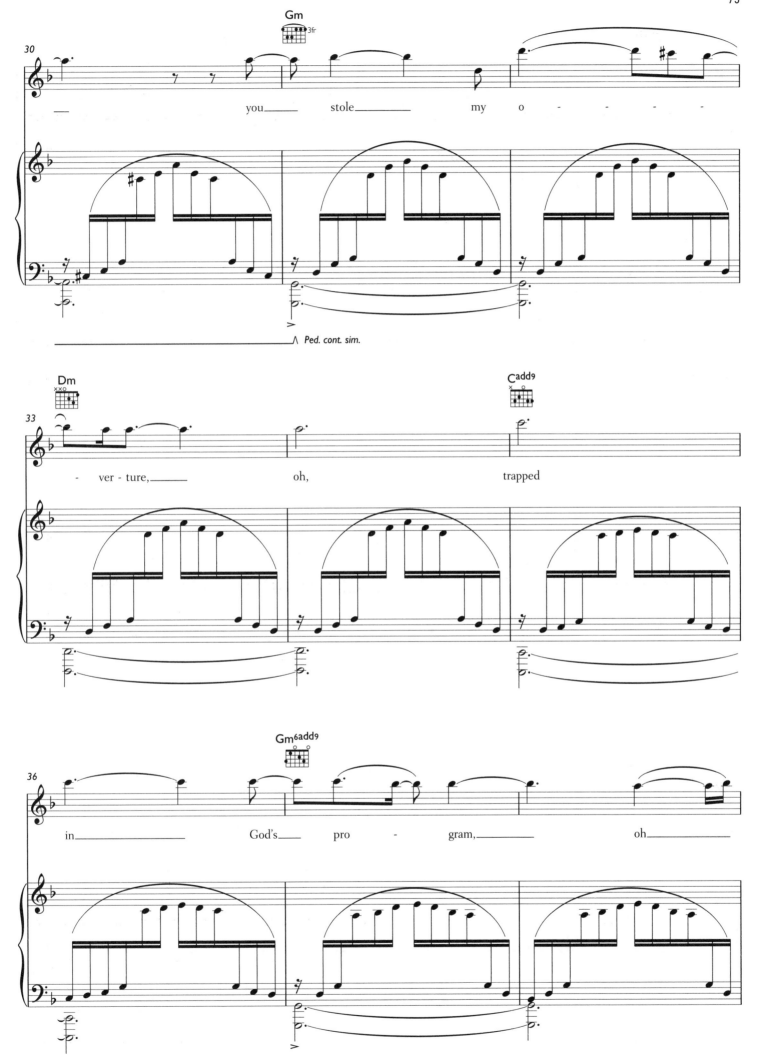

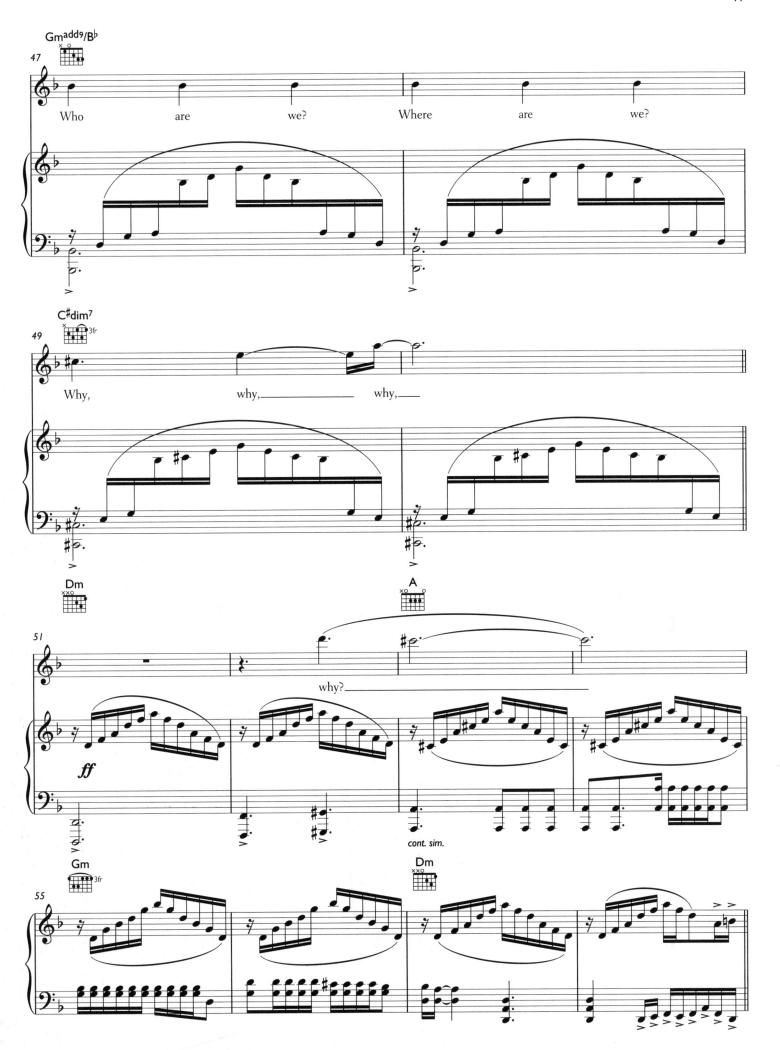

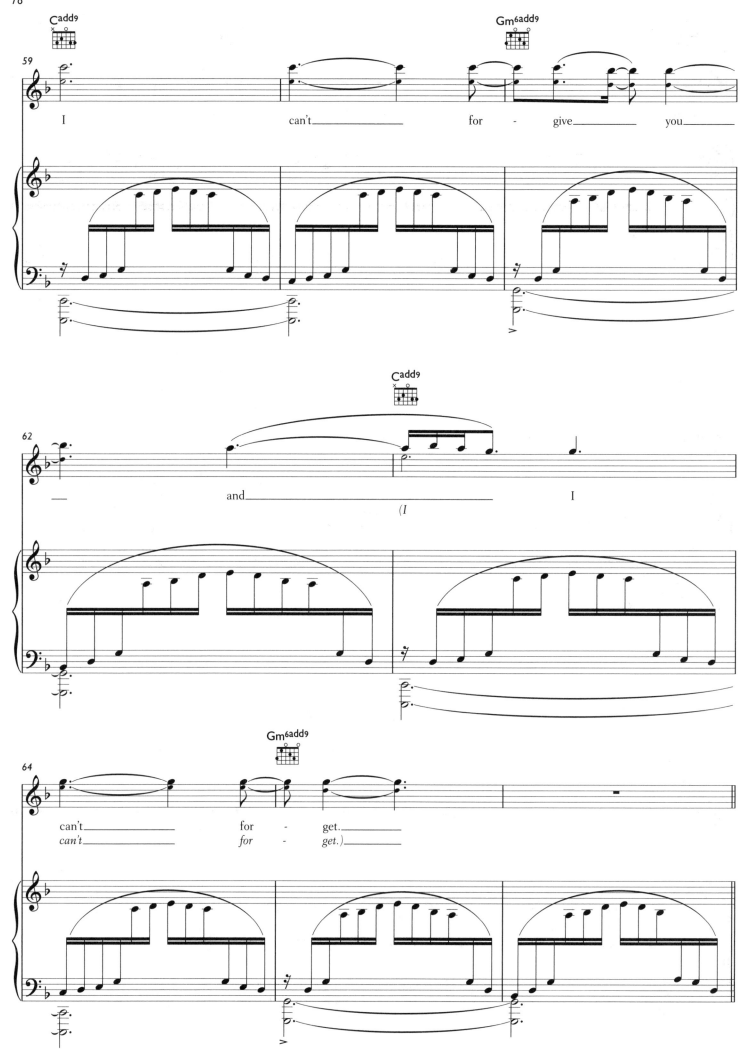

EXOGENESIS: SYMPHONY PART II (CROSS POLLINATION)

Words and Music by Matthew Bellamy

Spread, our codes _____ to the stars,

you must res - cue us all.

1. Tell us, what is your fi - nal wish? Now we know _____ you can
2. Tell us, what is your fi - nal wish? We will tell _____ it

EXOGENESIS: SYMPHONY PART III (REDEMPTION)

Words and Music by Matthew Bellamy